CHRONICLE OF AMERICA™

COLONIAL TIMES

1600–1700

JOY MASOFF

SCHOLASTIC REFERENCE

History Advisors:
Mary Beth Norton
M.D. Alger Professor
of American History
Cornell University

Robert Stremme
Elementary School and
College Educator

Library of Congress
Cataloging-in-Publication Data

Masoff, Joy, 1951– · Colonial times, 1600–1700 / by Joy Masoff. · p. cm.—-(Chronicle of America) · Includes bibliographical references (p.) and index. · Summary: Re-creates early American settlements by describing in words and pictures various aspects of the colonists' lives, including work, food, clothing, shelter, religion, and relationships with Native Americans. · 1. United States—History—Colonial period, ca. 1600–1775—Juvenile literature. · 2. United States—History—Colonial period, ca. 1600–1775—Pictorial works—Juvenile literature. · [1.United States—History—Colonial period, ca. 1600–1775.] I. Title. II. Series. · E188.M385 · 2000 · 99-056243 · 973.2—dc21 · CIP
ISBN 0-439-05107-X
10 9 8 7 6 5 4 3
02 03 04
Printed in Mexico 49
First printing, August 2000

TABLE OF CONTENTS

★

The story of America is about much more than boring dates and long names!

You are about to leave the present to set sail for a strange and wondrous place.

Travel back to America as it was in the 1600s as you set off on…

A GREAT ADVENTURE

See for yourself what life was really like when the first European settlers rowed onto America's shores. Stand alongside the Native Americans watching those odd-looking strangers arrive. Sail across the rough seas with the young Africans who were kidnapped and forced to work for strangers half a world away.

Find out how it felt to spend two months at sea in a space the size of a closet, to wash in water so cold you had to break through a layer of ice before you could use it, to crawl out from underneath a cozy quilt in the middle of the night and run outside when nature called.

Take a 400-year-long journey back in time and discover a land that's so very different from the one we live in today.

Grab a grown-up and try your hand at some early colonial crafts. Eat like a Pilgrim. Make a sailor's bracelet.

Only when you understand what it was like to live during the past, can you begin to understand how we got to where we are now.

Enjoy the trip!

How would you feel if you sat down to a dinner of meat loaf with maggots?

Would you be hungry if you knew that your meal would probably be

followed by a really upset stomach?

What does spoiled food have to do with America's history?

Well…it all began with a hunk of rotten meat.

Meat that needed spices to cover the bad taste. Spices that Columbus set out in

search of, on a journey that would take him…

ACROSS THE SEA OF GLOOM

Who found America? Probably a couple of hungry pre-historic hunters in search of something wooly *and* mammoth to eat—folks who hiked over from Asia at a time when the two continents were still connected. They had the new land all to themselves for well over 20,000 years, until around the year 1000, when a boatload of Scandinavian sailors stumbled ashore and tried to put down roots in what is now part of Canada.

These Vikings lasted about a year before they gave up and headed home. After that, no one but some stray fishers bothered with the hidden land surrounded by great oceans until Christopher Columbus took a deep breath, offered up a prayer, and sailed off across the Sea of Gloom.

That's what the Atlantic Ocean was called back in 1492. Old sailors swore there were monsters in the sea that could swallow up a ship in one gulp, but Christopher Columbus was a risk-taker. He had faith in himself, his sailors, and his ships. He believed he could reach the Orient—land of spice and silk—by going west instead of east. His confidence paid off. He "discovered" a new continent.

When Columbus returned home, word spread fast through the Spanish courts and across Europe. There was gold. There were jewels. There were fabulous riches everywhere. Soon, explorers from every seafaring country in Europe set off to claim a piece of this new world. They felt that the riches of the mysterious new land were theirs for the taking. Nothing was going to stop them.

THE BEST AND WORST OF TIMES
★

This beautiful country was a land where people made mistakes, where too much was "not fair," and where greed made people do bad things. Yet it was also a land of new friendships, where over time, people began to accept and understand the ways of others from different, distant lands.

Here is the story of how and why so much went right—or wrong—in the very early days of America, the years after Columbus returned to Spain with news of his amazing "discovery."

WHERE THREE CONTINENTS COLLIDED
★

Something special happened in the Americas, something that set this land apart from the rest of the world. It was here that a mix of adventurous European settlers, brave Native Americans, and Africa's strongest men and women—hundreds of different cultures, languages and beliefs—were stirred into something new and wonderful.

Things that did not exist in America, like horses and metal, were unloaded from Europeans' boats. Things that did not exist in Europe, like tomatoes and potatoes, were shipped back from the new settlements. And life on both sides of the ocean was changed forever.

Would you be able to say good-bye to your friends and family…maybe forever? For some people, the choice to leave their homes and loved ones was easy. Life was hard in the Old World. The cities were overcrowded and there was sickness in the air. If you were born poor, you stayed poor. Sometimes the best chance you had was…

RUNNING AWAY FROM HOME

Europe in the 1600s was a nasty place to be. A terrible war dragged on and on…lasting for 30 years. Thousands were killed, all in the name of religion. There were serious crop failures and food was scarce. And to add to the misery, in one year alone, 41,000 people died in London when a plague struck.

To some people—the poor, orphans, and criminals—the New World represented their only chance to escape from a doomed life.

Now, to hear people talking back then you would think that only "bad people" left for America. But the truth was that plenty of folks with courage and big dreams decided that the adventure of a new life was exactly what they wanted.

In time, postmasters and printers, artists and shopkeepers, soldiers and shoemakers, all packed up their belongings and sailed west to America. Most were city dwellers. Only a few knew much about farming, which would present problems when they first arrived on America's shores. Leaving was scary and exciting all at the same time.

6

PULLED TO A NEW WORLD...

In Europe in the 1600s, the family you were born into determined the way your life would turn out. If your father was a duke, your life would be pretty decent. If you were the child of a farmer, you became a farmer, too. For many people, the choice to leave Europe was made because they felt trapped. Coming to America offered them a chance to make something of their lives. Any hope was better than none. One sixteen-year-old boy left because his father beat him. A young man left to cure a broken heart. A few fearless, feisty women came because they wanted to find husbands. Everyone believed they would find happiness on America's shores.

PUSHED FROM THE OLD

Many were pushed out of their homes because they couldn't worship God in the way they wanted to.

The most famous of the religious travelers were the Pilgrims. But they were not alone. The Huguenots, a religious sect in France, also suffered greatly. Many were killed as war ripped across the continent. Churches were burned—all in the name of God. In Spain, in the same year Columbus sailed across the Atlantic, every Jewish person in the country was told to leave. For some, it was the New World...or death.

A ROYAL PAIN

The King of England was a very powerful man, a man you didn't want to make mad. But that's exactly what a group of people called the Puritans did. They were called Puritans because they wanted to "purify" the Church of England. In those days, the church, led by the king, had a lot of power. One hundred years earlier, the Church of England had broken away from the Roman Catholic Church. The new church was supposed to be very different from the Catholic Church. The Puritans did not think it was. They called the grand cathedrals "dens of lazy, loitering lubbards," and the prayer book a thing "picked out of the Pope's chamber pot." That kind of talk can get people in trouble. The king at the time, James I, told them to stop saying bad things, or leave. So a group of Puritans, called Separatists, fled to Holland. They stayed there for 12 years. When the opportunity to start a new colony in America presented itself, they jumped at the chance!

HOW TO GET TO AMERICA

Let's suppose that you are a poor chimney sweep in England. If you have no money, how are you supposed to get across the ocean? Well, not only the poor knew that there was money to be made in America. Wealthy folks—people who didn't want to leave their comfy homes and their friends behind—still wanted to profit from the riches of the New World. They started businesses to explore and exploit the land across the sea. If you agreed to become an indentured servant and work for them without being paid over a period of time, usually five to seven years, they would pay your way over from Europe and keep you clothed and housed. At the end of that time, your boss would give you clothes, tools, and perhaps a piece of land. That was how most people made the trip across the sea.

PACKING FOR A NEW LIFE

No new arrival in America could manage without packing some pretty odd things. There were no grocery stores in the New World in the early 1600s, so the first settlers brought pigs, cows, goats, and sheep. They brought tools for building and gardening. They gathered seeds from their favorite plants and veggies. And they usually took one beloved piece of furniture, often a chest, stuffed with as much as it would hold. Try fitting all that in a suitcase! Then, it was time for one last hug for friends and family before the walk up the gangplank. The ship would be leaving soon.

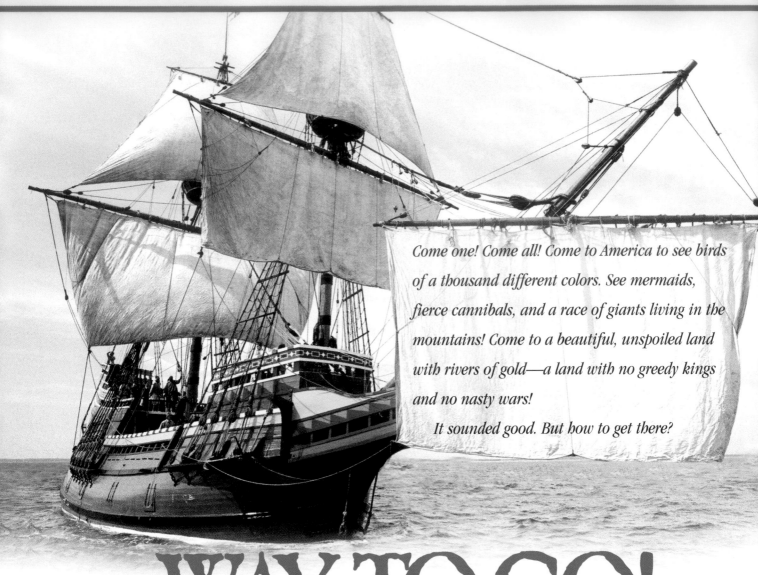

Come one! Come all! Come to America to see birds of a thousand different colors. See mermaids, fierce cannibals, and a race of giants living in the mountains! Come to a beautiful, unspoiled land with rivers of gold—a land with no greedy kings and no nasty wars!

It sounded good. But how to get there?

WAY TO GO!

Frustration. Poverty. Disease. War. *That* was the way of life for most people in the Old World. Rivers of gold and mermaids sounded a lot better than hunger and hopelessness.

COMING TO AMERICA
★

A long cruise on a big ship sounds nice. Shuffleboard, lots to eat, a deck full of lounge chairs. Unfortunately, a voyage to America in the 1600s wasn't anything like that.

What was it like? Imagine standing in a small crowded elevator. Now, pretend that everyone and everything in it is damp or wet. It smells like dirty gym socks and there are babies crying and mothers wailing.

The ship keeps going up and down, way too fast. Imagine that three people have just thrown up. All you can hear is moaning and creaking and you believe that at any second the entire ship will be ripped apart by the fierce seas.

Now, endure all that for two to four long months like the first people to come to America aboard ships such as the *Susan Constant,* bound for Virginia, and the *Mayflower,* which ended up in Massachusetts.

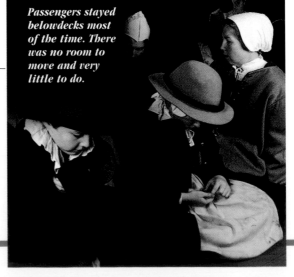

Passengers stayed belowdecks most of the time. There was no room to move and very little to do.

BULLY ON BOARD

The *Mayflower* was one of the most famous ships to make the crossing to the New World. It left England on September 6, 1620, along with another vessel called the *Speedwell*. Unfortunately, the *Speedwell* didn't speed well at all. It developed a huge leak and turned back to port.

On board the *Mayflower*, 102 passengers, 3 of whom were expecting babies, crammed into a space the size of two classrooms. A chill was in the air and the cold of winter was on its way. Days stretched into weeks and then months with nothing to do but sit squashed in a small space. And one particular seaman was horribly mean to the passengers, making fun of them and bullying them. He would yell that they'd be better off tossed over the side.

William Bradford, a passenger who would go on to become the second governor of what would come to be Massachusetts Bay Colony, wrote in his history of the Pilgrims, "But it pleased God before they came half seas over, to smite this young man with a grievous disease, of which he died in a desperate manner, and so was himself the first that was thrown overboard."

The passengers took this as a clear sign that God was on their side!

SURPRISING HISTORY

More than just the Pilgrims came over on the *Mayflower*. The settlers brought cockroaches, flies, and gray rats from the Old World to the New.

It took 2,500 trees to build a ship about the size of the *Mayflower*. As more and more ships were built to come to the New World, the forests of Europe almost disappeared.

FOOD THAT MOVED

Mealtimes at sea were another test of will. Many passengers preferred to eat in the dark. That way they couldn't see the bugs that were crawling in their food.

Hardtack, well-named because it was as hard as a rock and as tasty as rusty metal, was the ship's mainstay. Its proper name was ship's biscuit and it was made from dried bread that had been crumbled, mixed with a little water, then re-baked. Its hardness guaranteed that it couldn't spoil. Alas, it also made it impossible to eat. You had to break it up with a brick, place a hunk of the crumbled stuff in your cheek, and wait for your saliva to soften it. In later years hardtack would come to be known as "worm castles" because weevils and maggots always found their way into the stuff.

There was usually some meat or fish soaking in a big barrel full of brine—extra-salty water. Brine was so salty that people used to dip their food *in the ocean* to rinse off the salty taste! Cooking happened only when the water was calm. It was dangerous to have a fire on board in rough seas.

By the time the *Mayflower* anchored, the weather had turned damp and chilly. And as bad as life had been aboard ship, life in the New World would prove even harder.

TIED UP IN KNOTS

Sometimes sailing was hard work. But other times, when the winds were calm, it was really boring. So sailors busied themselves with small bits of leftover rope, trying to see who could come up with the most complicated knots. Every sailor worth his salt had a Turk's Head bracelet. Here's how to make a simple version of one:

Cut 7 lengths of string each 12" long. Knot at the top.

Tuck the knotted end into a slit cut into a piece of cardboard. Keeping the strands flat, divide as shown.

Braid, keeping the strands flat. Knot at the bottom. Remove from the cardboard and tie around your wrist!

A yellow string was used here for clarity. Make your bracelet all white, or multicolored!

You've been on the ship for two months. You have almost no food or fresh water left.

Your clothing is filthy, stiff with dirt and sweat.

You want to get off…right now!

Then, just ahead, shimmering in the early morning light, you see it.

Land at last!

I SEE AMERICA!

One of the first people to settle in America described it as a scary wilderness full of wild beasts and even wilder men. But in truth, it wasn't like that at all.

Most of the coastline had already been settled by the first Americans—the Native Americans. For centuries they had been clearing acres and acres of land and planting crops. The America the newcomers found was anything *but* untamed wilderness!

The first Europeans to come to the New World found already cleared fields and abandoned Native American villages where they could take temporary shelter. The Pilgrims were even greeted by two Native Americans who spoke English, learned from trading with the fishermen and trappers who had been coming to the New World for a hundred years!

The newcomers found strange and wonderful foods and flowers…wild strawberries, tomatoes, and persimmons. They found brooks and streams so filled with fish that one person said it was impossible to cross without stepping on a fish. There were flocks of wild turkeys, upward of four and five hundred, running across the meadows. And there were so many ducks that when they migrated the sun was blotted out.

But there was one problem with all that bounty. The new arrivals didn't know what to do first. Few had weapons. Most of them were weak or ill from their long sea journey. Every decision seemed so hard to make.

In Jamestown, Virginia, some of the new arrivals were "gentlemen" who didn't want to get their hands dirty. In Plymouth, the Pilgrims' new settlement, the settlers were expecting mild weather year-round. They were stunned and surprised when the first brutally cold New England winter hit.

SURPRISING HISTORY

Most people believe that America was named for Amerigo Vespucci, an Italian geographer who made several voyages to—and more important, maps of—the New World. The maps bore his name in big letters across the bottoms. But some believe that this land got its name from the Vikings. *Omme-rike* means "the remote land" in the Norse language!

WHERE SHOULD WE LIVE?
★

Picking out a site for a settlement was the biggest challenge the new arrivals faced and deadly mistakes were made doing that. Take Jamestown. It seemed like a wonderful place for a town. There was a deep-water harbor—perfect for tying up big ships. Jamestown was tucked far enough up the James River that it was well-hidden from Spanish soldiers trying to keep the New World all to themselves. It was a semi-island protected on three sides by water and marsh. But this paradise would turn out to be a death trap—a swamp with foul drinking water. Mosquitoes carrying the disease malaria swarmed around by the thousands. Badly draining soil led to constant outbreaks of diseases like dysentery. But the new arrivals did not know any of that! They thought Jamestown was perfect.

Depending on where they landed, some new arrivals found curious Native Americans waiting to greet them as they rowed to shore. Others got a less cordial welcome and had to fire off their ship's cannon to settle things down.

THE NEW LAND'S GREAT GIFTS
★

The Europeans knew, from the moment they set foot on America's soil, that things were going to be very different in this strange new place. There were no cities, no grand churches, no shops. They realized that they were all alone, far from the life they had known. Everything seemed bigger and wilder—tall forests of great trees and animals in such abundance as to be almost frightening. They had arrived safely on America's shores. Now, the hard part was beginning. Survival!

The first Americans had already cleared hundreds of acres of land before the first Europeans arrived.

The fort at Jamestown offered a feeling of safety for the settlers. But the same fort that kept the Native Americans out, kept the settlers imprisoned. That would almost prove the colony's undoing!

THE MYSTERY OF THE LOST COLONY

The first English colonists—120 people, including 17 women and 2 children—had arrived in America in 1587 with high hopes. They landed in Roanoke, Virginia, to start a new settlement. The leader of the colonists, John White, had to go back to England. When he returned to America, the village was deserted. On a nearby tree, he discovered the word CROATAN carved into the trunk. No one knows what happened, but many believe that the settlers died or chose to go live with the Croatan Indians. White never found them and to this day Roanoke is known as "The Lost Colony."

How would you feel if strange-looking people suddenly showed up in your backyard? Would you be surprised? Angry? Interested? Would you help them out? Share your food and shelter? Those were questions that Native Americans had to answer because…

THEY WERE HERE FIRST!

By the time Columbus came ashore, there were already millions of people here—living in sprawling settlements, building great monuments, spread out across the entire continent. The New World was really very old.

For years people have lumped the Native Americans together as one big group. But nothing could be further from the truth. In the land that would one day be called "America," there were more than three hundred different nations, each with its own customs and styles. There were 143 languages and a thousand dialects being spoken, each as different as French is from Chinese. Some Native American nations survived by fishing, some by hunting, some by farming. Certain groups hated other groups and fought constantly. Their differences were so great that they didn't think of themselves as one people. If they had, and joined together to fight off the Europeans, America would never have been colonized.

The arrival of the Europeans changed things. Some groups welcomed the new arrivals. Others sensed danger from the moment the ships sailed into their harbors. As the colonists' numbers grew, along with their demands for land, the Native Americans did what they had to do to defend their homes. War was waged. People died. Some Native Americans found themselves forced into slavery.

It was warm and cozy inside a Native American's longhouse, even in the coldest weather—much warmer than in the Europeans' wooden houses.

SURPRISING HISTORY

Of our 50 states, 26 have Native American names. Did you know that Texas means "friend" and that Kentucky means "planted field"? Miami and Chicago are just two American cities with Native American names!

Thousands of Native American words became a part of our language—words like skunk, chipmunk, and barbecue.

Most of our major roadways and cities are built on the sites of what were originally Native American towns and pathways.

LET'S MAKE A DEAL

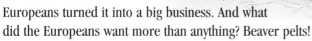

★

"I'll give you some fish if you give me some corn." "I have extra baskets but I need some deer skin." Trading had always been a way of life for the Native Americans. But the Europeans turned it into a big business. And what did the Europeans want more than anything? Beaver pelts!

During the 1600s, the only heat came from fireplaces. In the chilly countries of Europe, staying toasty was easier if you had a warm hat and coat. Beaver fur was silky, waterproof, and very warm. And there were lots of beavers in America.

However, because of the great demand, there soon were hardly any beavers left to hunt. Wars were started over the buck-toothed creatures!

The first Americans were enchanted by the Europeans' metal things—their strong knives and fishhooks, their sturdy cooking pots that stood up to heat better than clay, and especially their guns. Trading food, furs, and land for these things became a way of life.

A DEADLY TRADE

★

There were other things being exchanged besides furs and guns—deadly things like smallpox and measles. The Native Americans had never been exposed to these killer microbes. Their bodies had not developed an ability to fight them. Disease took a terrible toll, far worse than any weapons. Three-quarters of the Native American population fell sick and died from the colonists' new germs. Whole villages were wiped out. That's the reason why some colonists arriving from Europe found many Native American towns completely empty.

BATTLE CRY

★

The Powhatan in Virginia…the Timucua in Florida…the Wampanoag in Massachusetts… these were some of the first nations to have to deal with the permanent invasion of the Europeans. In time, their struggle to hold on to their way of life would be a struggle all the Native American nations would experience. Thousands would die. All would suffer. And this story would not have a happy ending.

FROM TEPEES TO STONE CITIES

There were huge differences between Native American nations including the sorts of houses they lived in. Along the Atlantic coast, longhouses were covered with bark or woven mats. The Plains Indians lived in animal-skin tepees that could be rolled up and moved easily. Some Southwestern groups lived in stone cliff dwellings carved into mountainsides.

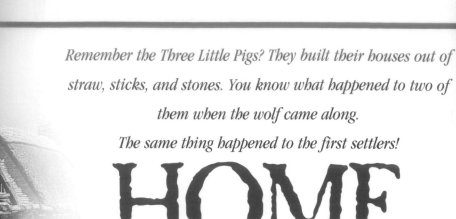

Remember the Three Little Pigs? They built their houses out of straw, sticks, and stones. You know what happened to two of them when the wolf came along. The same thing happened to the first settlers!

HOME SWEET HOME

After the long voyage from Europe, creating a place to live was one of the first things the newcomers to America had to do. But building a house is hard. It takes time to make it sturdy and secure. The new colonists didn't have time. They pitched makeshift tents on the shoreline and got to work.

When the protective walls of a fort were built, the settlers started on the next most important building in those days—a church! Yet more days passed for the colonists in their leaky, damp tents. Finally, the first houses were built, quickly…and badly. Storms easily blew those first houses apart. Fires often burned them to the ground. The settlers would simply sift through the ashes for the old nails, cut down a few more trees, and throw up another house.

HOUSES OF GRASS…

The Vikings dug pits in the earth, stuck in thick wooden posts, and covered it all with a layer of soil, complete with grass for a roof!

MUD AND STRAW…

In New Mexico, the Spanish settlers worked with adobe, a mixture of mud and straw that was baked into bricks.

It takes two to pit-saw. Colonists used these huge saws to turn a tree trunk into boards for building houses.

SAND AND TWIGS...

Jamestown's wattle and daub houses burned easily. Fires destroyed the town every few years.

THICK TREES...

New arrivals from Sweden brought the log cabin style with them. These cabins were much warmer and cozier than wooden board houses—stronger, too!

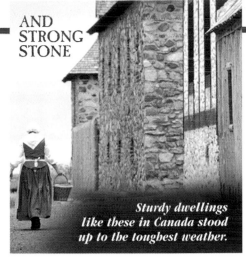

STICKS AND STONES

If it was lying around on the ground, it was used to build a house. Reeds from the fields, mud from the riverbanks, and roughly cut logs were the raw ingredients needed.

Most houses were begun the same way—by driving four thick posts deep into the ground. But then, depending on where the settlers ended up, house-building differed.

In the Southwest, the Native Americans taught the Spanish colonists how to use adobe. The thick, earthen walls kept them warm when it grew chilly, and cool 'neath the hot summer sun.

Along the eastern coast, houses were built of wattle and daub—thin slats of wood were woven horizontally through a vertical frame. Clay soil was mixed with water, sand, and straw. The thick paste was slathered over the wood and allowed to dry. Up in New England, where the weather was more extreme, colonists took advantage of the thick forests. They cut boards from tree trunks and nailed them over the wattle and daub, each board slightly overlapping the one beneath it.

ROOM SERVICE

The first houses the colonists built had only one big room. They were damp and dark inside, the floors made of packed-down dirt. There was no playroom or bathroom—or bedrooms for that matter. A few lucky folks had chamber pots, bowls that you used to answer nature's call without having to go outside. But when most settlers had to urinate, outdoors was where they went.

SURPRISING HISTORY

Thatch, the bundles of reed stems used to cover roofs, is extremely durable. But it takes over a million reeds to roof a small house. It took weeks to gather enough razor-sharp thatch bundles to complete a house. Fortunately, a good thatch will keep a house dry for 25 years.

HOUSE WARMERS

Every house had a big fireplace—a combination stove and heat source. But these fireplaces were drafty and let in more cold air than they heated. Beds were rare. Most people had a mattress that got rolled up in the morning and stored away for the day. Snazzier houses had a storage loft, reached by a ladder, where a lucky person might get some privacy.

BUILT TO LAST

It would take many years, but eventually decent homes did get built. People got tired of rebuilding their always-falling-down, always-catching-on-fire houses. They finally had some money and could afford more expensive building materials, such as brick. Their roots had been put down. America was now their home, sweet home.

Feeling a little hungry? In America's early days, food was serious business.

Men killed for it, stole it, guarded it like gold.

Every meal meant a lot of work. Wheat had to be picked, peas had to be picked,

chickens had to have their feathers picked. And you

sometimes had to pick the goat hairs out of the milk. We were indeed a nation of...

PICKY EATERS

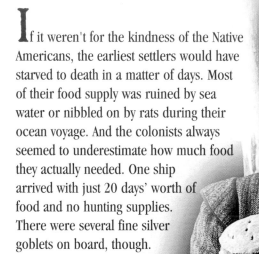

If it weren't for the kindness of the Native Americans, the earliest settlers would have starved to death in a matter of days. Most of their food supply was ruined by sea water or nibbled on by rats during their ocean voyage. And the colonists always seemed to underestimate how much food they actually needed. One ship arrived with just 20 days' worth of food and no hunting supplies. There were several fine silver goblets on board, though.

Some ships pulled up to America's shores with nothing left to eat! After months at sea with no fresh food, is it any wonder that some early settlers were forced to turn to cannibalism?

EAT LIKE A PILGRIM: CORN CAKES

Take three cups of water and stir in one cup of coarse cornmeal grits. Simmer until all the water is absorbed. When cool, turn the mixture onto a floured work surface and shape it into two round, flat cakes. Bake at 375° for 45 minutes.

After you've discovered what true early-settler food really tastes like, you might find you'd like to top these with a little jam or butter.

FOOD FIGHTS!
★

Arriving in Jamestown in the early spring of 1607, the settlers faced a major problem. They had chosen a low, marshy spot to build their town on, not realizing that their drinking water was foul and the region was in the middle of a severe drought. It had not rained in weeks.

In addition, the "gentlemen" who had come over didn't want to get their hands dirty by planting. That was a farmer's work! In fact, they didn't want to do much of anything but hang out and play cards. Fighting broke out among the colonists. Finally, some settlers grudgingly planted wheat and vegetables. But since no one knew much about farming, the crops didn't do very well.

Summer arrived with unbearable heat and no rain. The crops shriveled. The colonists grew sick from lack of food and insect-borne diseases—too sick to tend to their meager gardens. They ended up fighting over some leftover barley from the voyage. That barley, now six months old, was more worms than grain. Almost half of the settlers died that summer in the swampy heat. The colonists had to learn to cooperate if they were going to survive in this strange, new place!

WHAT'S TO EAT?

★

The new arrivals survived by learning to eat the Native American way. They now ate corn and squash. In the Southwest, they discovered how yummy tortillas were. Native Americans showed the colonists how to trap fish and eat oysters. They taught the settlers how to fertilize the fields and when to harvest.

A FEAST OF THANKSGIVING

★

Open flames while cooking were always a danger. Skirts easily caught on fire. So did houses!

What was placed on the tables of the early settlers? Breakfast was usually hasty pudding, a watery oatmeal or cornmeal mush, served with a little cheese and some bread. That was washed down by a glass of beer or hard cider. Milk simply wasn't drunk. Breakfast leftovers were fed to the chickens—everyone had a few pecking out in the yard. Butter had to be churned, a process that took hours.

Lunch was usually pottage, a thick stew of vegetables and other odd bits. It was served with cornbread and, perhaps, some sliced wild turkey. There were no forks, just spoons and knives. Meat and greens were eaten with your hands. And since lunch was so yummy, pottage was served again for dinner.

Occasionally, depending on the time of year, melons and beans made it onto the menu. Cod, bass, and eels joined wild turkeys and pheasant on the plate. In the first years in the New World the Pilgrims ate so much lobster that they grew sick of it. They decided that it was perfect as pig food!

The pursuit of food filled the day. Water had to be drawn in buckets from the stream. Wood had to be gathered and fires had to be stoked. The winters were so cold that goats and chickens were moved right into the house to keep them from turning into frozen food.

Food, and the lack of it, almost brought the first settlements down. But when it was plentiful, food would form the centerpiece for the great feast that became our holiday of Thanksgiving, first celebrated in the autumn of 1621.

America was finally becoming a land of plenty.

Kids stood at mealtimes. Chairs were for grown-ups only.

THE STARVING TIME

Sometimes there was no food at all. In Jamestown, the winter of 1609–10 was bitter cold. The colonists found themselves in trouble. They had angered the Powhatan Indians to the point where they had no choice but to stay inside their fort. Unfortunately, their cows, chickens, and pigs were outside. Soon they were forced to eat their pets. They ate rats, snakes, and horsehide. One man was put to death for eating his dead wife. People dug up bodies from the graveyard. By winter's end, 90 percent of the colonists had died. The survivors couldn't wait to leave Jamestown and the settlement was almost abandoned, all because of food.

There were "starving times" in every one of the first European settlements. And too often, in this land of plenty, people went to their graves for lack of something to eat.

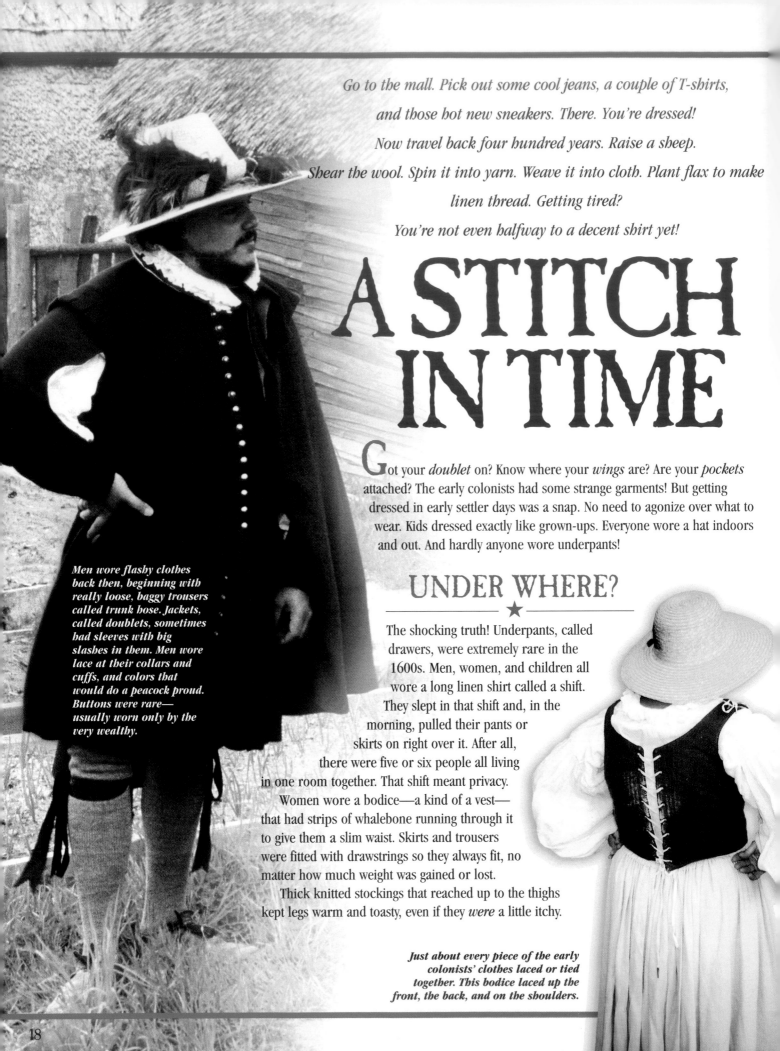

Go to the mall. Pick out some cool jeans, a couple of T-shirts, and those hot new sneakers. There. You're dressed!

Now travel back four hundred years. Raise a sheep. Shear the wool. Spin it into yarn. Weave it into cloth. Plant flax to make linen thread. Getting tired?

You're not even halfway to a decent shirt yet!

A STITCH IN TIME

Got your *doublet* on? Know where your *wings* are? Are your *pockets* attached? The early colonists had some strange garments! But getting dressed in early settler days was a snap. No need to agonize over what to wear. Kids dressed exactly like grown-ups. Everyone wore a hat indoors and out. And hardly anyone wore underpants!

Men wore flashy clothes back then, beginning with really loose, baggy trousers called trunk hose. Jackets, called doublets, sometimes had sleeves with big slashes in them. Men wore lace at their collars and cuffs, and colors that would do a peacock proud. Buttons were rare—usually worn only by the very wealthy.

UNDER WHERE?

★

The shocking truth! Underpants, called drawers, were extremely rare in the 1600s. Men, women, and children all wore a long linen shirt called a shift. They slept in that shift and, in the morning, pulled their pants or skirts on right over it. After all, there were five or six people all living in one room together. That shift meant privacy.

Women wore a bodice—a kind of a vest— that had strips of whalebone running through it to give them a slim waist. Skirts and trousers were fitted with drawstrings so they always fit, no matter how much weight was gained or lost.

Thick knitted stockings that reached up to the thighs kept legs warm and toasty, even if they *were* a little itchy.

Just about every piece of the early colonists' clothes laced or tied together. This bodice laced up the front, the back, and on the shoulders.

THE HIP-PY LOOK

★

In the 1600s, the "in" style for women was to have teeny little waists. One way to make the waist look smaller was to make the hips look bigger. To do that, women always wore a bum roll—a big, thick wad of padding tied around the hips. Over that, women wore petticoats. But these were meant to be seen. If it was cold, they layered on three or four. An apron topped those petticoats. Women always wore one!

Clothing was scarce. Most settlers had only two or three sets of clothes. And for about the first 20 or 30 years in the New World, they weren't even able to make new ones. It took too much time…time that was needed to grow food and build homes. It wasn't until the middle of the century that people were able to begin to weave cloth. Clothes were so valuable they were left to friends and loved ones when people died.

MAKE-IT-YOURSELF

★

For a long time, clothing was brought over from Europe. But in time, the colonists began to make it themselves, using wool, flax (a kind of plant used to make linen), and leather.

Woolen cloth was made by shearing sheep, pulling out the dirty clumps, then carding the wool—combing it over and over again until it got long and stringy. Next, it was ready to be spun into yarn on a spinning wheel and woven into cloth on a loom. Flax was prepared much the same way, soaking and beating the plant fibers until they got soft and stringy. Both took weeks to make!

THE COLORS OF THE NEW WORLD

Forget all the paintings you've seen of the Pilgrims dressed only in dull black or gray. The very early settlers wore lots of bright colors—reds, yellows, and purples. They used flowers, berries, and even bugs, to dye cloth they brought with them from Europe. Why not try your hand at it?

Marigolds and goldenrod give lovely yellow shades. Ragweed will make a beautiful rich green. Mulberries make pink and elderberries make blues and lavenders. Onion skin gives a soft, pale yellow. Begin by soaking the flowers, leaves, or roots in a cup of hot water. Next, add a teaspoon of cream of tartar to the liquid. Then, soak some cut-up squares of old T-shirts in the different "brews" and compare the colors.

SURPRISING HISTORY

Women used to wear their pockets dangling from a string around their waists. Inside pockets weren't invented until the 1700s.

Until the age of about seven, boys and girls dressed alike—boys wore skirts!
Jackets often had wings, flaps that extended over the shoulders. Sleeves laced into the wings and could be removed in warm weather, or if a sleeve got dirty and needed a quick wash.

19

Bored with all your games? Try passing the time with nothing but

a few sticks and a rock or two. Sister or brother getting on your nerves?

Imagine being stuck inside one small room with your entire family for a solid month.

From daybreak to day's end, come spend…

A DAY IN A CHILD'S LIFE

No school? Sounds good, but children in the first settlements still had to learn how to read, write, and add. And they had to do it in between feeding chickens, working in the fields, churning butter, dipping candles, and watching their brothers and sisters. Moms and dads were the teachers and the principals, too. There was no goofing off!

Each day was filled with chores and more chores. Cows to milk, fields to tend to, meals to help prepare. *That* was a typical day in a child's life.

AS EASY AS A,B,C
★

How did kids learn to read? Some turned to a horn book, which really wasn't a book at all. It was a wooden paddle that had a piece of paper tacked to it, covered with the letters of the alphabet, simple combinations of vowels and consonants, and the Lord's Prayer. And the horn? A thin layer shaved off a cow's horn protected the paper from grubby little fingers. Children used a sharp stick and traced over the shapes of each letter until they had them down pat.

3+3+3=9
★

Clever parents knew how to make math fun. Some kids learned how to count with the game of ninepin. It worked like this: Nine wooden cones were set up, either in a straight row or in three rows of three. The object of the game was to be the first person to knock down exactly 31 pins. If you knocked down more than 31 pins, you'd next have to try to get 39. If you missed 39, the next winning number was 48. If you knocked down more than 48, the next winning number was 57, and so on. If you couldn't count, you couldn't play, could you?

Baby walkers helped little ones take their first steps. Of course, they could only go forward and backward!

MORE MATH FUN

★

There were other nifty ways to master math. Pilgrim parents taught kids how to add by using a game made from a wooden box divided into five alleys. Each alley had a number written on it. Players rolled a small ball from the bottom into one of the alleys. The person who had the highest score after ten rolls was the winner.

WRITE LIKE THE FIRST SETTLERS

Feathers make great pens. But before you can write with them you have to make a nib—another word for a point. Grab a grown-up and give it a try.

Cut the shaft of the feather on an angle.

Then, shape the tip as shown here.

Make a short vertical cut at the tip.

A pen without ink is useless. In the 1600s folks made ink from walnuts, which they ground, then boiled. The brew was mixed with vinegar and a little salt.

A LOT OF WORK...

★

From the age of three, a child was expected to work around the house. Simple chores, such as wood gathering, kept little kids out of the way of busy moms and dads. For much of the day, kids rarely saw a grown-up.

Youngsters were given a level of freedom that would shock modern-day parents. John Adams, who would grow up to be a great leader and president, was given a rifle at the age of eight and with no adult supervision at all, spent days and days hunting ducks. Lucky ducks—he missed most of them!

There was no such thing as being a teenager in the 1600s. No generation gap. No fads. Styles did not change from year to year because there weren't any stores to tempt folks with new clothes. Kids followed closely in their parents' footsteps, learning from them and eventually becoming like them.

Girls learned how to cook and mend, keep a garden, and make medical potions. Boys learned how to build houses, clear fields, and shoot straight. They learned what they needed to know to survive. Living through the winter was more important than hanging out with your buddies.

The first proper school in America was started in 1635 in Boston, where there were enough children to make group learning possible. Harvard College was founded a year later. But for most children, the school of life was the only school in town.

SURPRISING HISTORY

Really big families were very common by the mid-to-late 1600s. Ben Franklin had 17 brothers and sisters. One well-known New England family had 26 children! Try getting into the bathroom with that many siblings standing in line in front of you!

A LITTLE PLAY

★

All work? No play? Of course not! Between all the chores and the learning, there was still time to play games. Kids rolled hoops and played quoits, a ring-toss game. They played checkers with light and dark stones. There were dominoes made of wood scraps and dolls to hug. Kids were still kids.

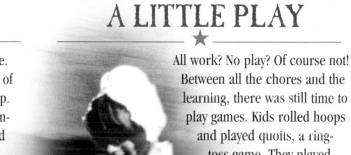

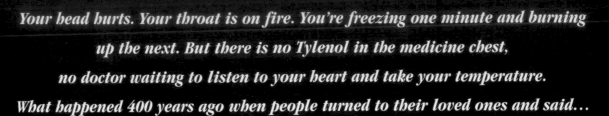

Your head hurts. Your throat is on fire. You're freezing one minute and burning up the next. But there is no Tylenol in the medicine chest, no doctor waiting to listen to your heart and take your temperature. What happened 400 years ago when people turned to their loved ones and said...

I FEEL SICK!

Getting sick was part of life back in the early days of America. Depending on where you lived, you might find yourself feeling rotten a lot of the time! In the first half of the 1600s, the new settlers who ended up in Virginia found themselves far sicker than those whose ships pulled up in the North. In the early days of the European settlements, 80 percent of the people who came to Virginia died once they got here. Here's what ailed them...

FLUX AND AGUE

★

Diseases had different names back then. The "runs" went by the name of the flux…or when it was really bad, "bloody flux." A person with an ague had a fever. There were slow agues, worm agues, and continual agues…and a lot of people *getting* agues. People believed that their illnesses were caused by bad things floating around in their blood. That being the case, there was one thing, and one thing only, to be done.

BLOOD BATHS

★

Bad blood had to be removed from the body. It was that simple. Every good doctor in the 1600s carried a lancet with him. It looked like a pocket knife and it was perfect for nicking open a vein and bleeding a person. About ten ounces was drawn (that's a little over a cup of blood). Most patients swore they felt better after. Oddly, a person who was unconscious never was bled.

Bloodletting was often followed by purging. We know it better as throwing up. Vile potions that made people vomit were taken to rid the body of any evil things that still might be lurking in it. One of the remedies, syrup of ipecac, is still used today in cases of accidental poisoning. Chances are there's some in your medicine cabinet. And speaking of medicine cabinets…

MAKE AN EARLY SETTLER BANDAGE

How much easier it would have been for the colonists if Band-Aids had existed back then! But, of course, they didn't. To make a dressing for a wound they had to scrape fibers off their clothes until they had a pile of lint.

You'll need a scrap of linen to get lint. Spread the fabric out so it's flat. Then, holding it firmly with one hand, start scraping with a butter knife. Small bits of fiber will come off the fabric. Pile it all up until you have a mound about the size of a teaspoon. How much time did it take?

SURPRISING HISTORY

Doctors weren't the only ones who could bleed a patient. Barbers also snipped veins in between snipping hair. They also pulled rotten teeth.

Calling the tooth fairy! One thing the colonists *did* have was lots of cavities. They loved sweets! In time, sugar from the Caribbean became easy to get and the Native Americans taught them how to extract maple syrup from trees.

Alas, there were no dentists to make the settlers brush and floss their teeth.

NATURE'S MEDICINE CHEST

★

Nowadays, pharmacists try to make medicine taste good. But in the 1600s, they believed it should taste bad. The worse it tasted, the better it was for you. Pity the poor kid who had to swallow a syrup made from wood lice! One popular remedy was an herb that smelled so bad, it was called "devil's dung." An oft-taken pill was made from deer dung and turpentine.

A well-stocked medicine chest might have these things: bear fat, garlic, horseradish, licorice, mustard, mint, nutmeg, vinegar, prickly pears, wax, violets, sumac, swamp lilies, sassafras, and peach blossoms. Every wife had a physick garden, in which she grew the plants needed to whip up a quick potion or a cure.

IS THERE A DOCTOR IN THE HOUSE?

★

There *were* a few medical men in the colonies. A doctor even came over on the *Mayflower*. The Native Americans shared many a medical cure with the new colonists. But in most cases, mom was the doctor back then. Some of those moms knew things that have stuck with us to this day. One of today's most useful medicines for treating heart disease originally came from a wise woman's garden. The leaves of the foxglove are now used to make the drug digitalis.

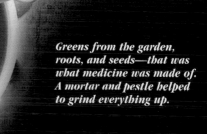

Greens from the garden, roots, and seeds—that was what medicine was made of. A mortar and pestle helped to grind everything up.

23

Arrows might come zinging through the air. You might find a bear drooling over your lunch. If you were a new colonist, you wouldn't be caught dead without a weapon of some sort 'cause without a gun, a sword, or a knife, chances were good you would *be caught…DEAD. No doubt about it. Guns were a must-have, especially when the call went out…*

READY. AIM. FIRE!

Well…what they actually said was, "Present. Give. Fire." Aiming was almost impossible with the guns that existed in the 1600s. But that didn't keep the new colonists from lugging matchlock muskets around whenever they left the safety of their forts.

TOP GUN

Matchlock muskets were awkward to carry and very heavy (close to 20 pounds). But if a colonist *did* manage to hit something when the musket was fired, it left a hole the size of a fist.

Muskets were useless for hunting since they were fired by a slow-burning piece of cord that smelled almost as bad as the gunpowder. Most savvy animals picked up on the scent and scampered to safety.

Scouring sticks at the ready, two Jamestown settlers prepare to fire a cannon. The man at the right is wearing a jack coat, a kind of lightweight armor, cooler to wear in the Virginia heat than metal armor.

SURPRISING HISTORY

If you think armor went out of style with the Knights of the Round Table, think again. Armor was the only thing standing between a colonist and a Native American's arrow. In the early 1600s, colonists lucky enough to have armor always wore it when the time came to fight.

ROUGH, TOUGH TIMES

It must have seemed as if the whole world was fighting in the 1600s. Wars went on for years and years. But war in those days was almost like a chess game. There were rules. You had to play fair. There was no hiding behind rocks. No sneaking out after dark. Armies lined up in neat rows opposite each other, close enough to see the whites of each other's eyes. When one team had had enough, everyone quit and went home.

But in America, that wasn't how the game was played. People hid behind trees. They shot after dark. During wartime, many Native American nations were determined to protect their lands from the enemy. If it meant picking off the new settlers one by one, that was fine with them. One colonist was even killed when he slipped off into the woods to answer nature's call.

The men of Jamestown and Spain's fort at St. Augustine in Florida depended on their big cannons to keep the enemy away. A cannon could shoot to a distance of a half mile!

RAG-TAG SOLDIERS

Most of the new arrivals in America had never held a gun in their hands. How were they to defend themselves? Males between the ages of sixteen and sixty had to join the militia, a kind of loosely formed army. Once a month, the men would grab their guns and head off for a muster, something like soccer practice, except war was what they were learning. No settlement existed without a militia. To do so would have meant death.

Sadly, the colonists' practicing would be very useful in the years to come. Battles erupted with the Native Americans all too often. So did fights with other European colonists. The Spanish fought the French and pushed them out of Florida. The English fought the Dutch and New Netherland became New York. The French and the Native Americans teamed up to wage war on the English settlers. Peace seemed a distant dream.

DRESSED TO KILL

This is what the well-dressed militiaman carried with him: Slung across his chest was a bandolier, a kind of belt from which dangled little wooden casks filled with gunpowder. He also had to carry a long stick called a scouring stick to push the gunpowder down toward the area where it could be lit. He would need a length of cord that was lit at one end to ignite the gunpowder. His gun was so heavy that he needed a forked stick called a musket rest to lean it on when he shot. And just in case it didn't work, a sword was a good backup.

WARFARE— THE NATIVE AMERICAN WAY

The Native Americans did not have guns when the Europeans first arrived, but they could inflict a great deal of damage with their bows and arrows, clubs, and tomahawks. The New England nations used long bows—some as tall as six feet! For up-close fighting, war clubs could be lethal weapons. They were made from the roots of trees, each bit of root sharpened to a knifelike point. These were replaced by the tomahawk, which the Native Americans got from European traders. But what they really wanted was muskets. By the late 1600s many groups were well supplied with them—leading to yet more death and destruction.

Cold mornings. Too many chores. Water frozen in the washbasin. Cows frozen in the fields. What did it take to be able to stand up to the rigors of such a difficult life? How did people ever manage to survive? Come spend one year with a typical family of early colonists and share their...

SEASONS OF PLENTY...

From spring's first flowers to summer's long, warm days...from fall's harvest to winter's bleakness, the seasons controlled the settlers' lives. The hot, humid, summer air of Virginia almost wiped out the first settlement in Jamestown. The Pilgrims barely survived the brutally cold New England winters. The Europeans had never seen a hurricane. They soon found out that the weather in the New World could be deadly.

SUMMER AND FALL
★

You might think of summer as a time to kick back and relax. But in the early colonies, summer was filled with hours of backbreaking work. Everybody became a farmer when they came to America. And everybody grew corn. It was the perfect plant because it fed both people and animals, was very hardy, and was easy to grow. Every single part of the plant could be used—husks to stuff mattresses, and cobs to make jar stoppers or corncob pipes.

The Native Americans taught the settlers to plant "when the oak leaves reached the size of a mouse's ears." Once the corn was up, other plants would be started in its shade—things like beans and pumpkin vines. Fruit trees would begin to bear fruits. Apples and peaches ended up as cider or wine. At harvest time, everyone got busy. There was a flurry of picking and drying and preserving. Hogs had to be slaughtered, and as the saying went, everything got used but the squeal. The intestines became sausage casings, while the bladder became a lard holder. The long tail hairs were used for sewing. The meat from four hogs, salted and stored in barrels, would last a family an entire winter. They would need every scrap of food they could gather as the days grew shorter.

SEASONS OF WANT

WINTER AND SPRING

Bitter cold days found the colonists sleeping in the fireplaces.

It was winter, with its biting cold, that killed. Staying warm through the bleak days required lots and lots of wood—wood that had to be gathered, chopped, dried, and split. People wore every garment they owned and existed on only dried or salted foods. They tried to stay warm by huddling around their hearths, but as one settler described it, "if you are not so close to the fire as almost to burn yourself, you cannot keep warm, for the wind blows through everywhere."

Nothing fresh to eat. Nothing to do. Days dragged on, and the woodpile got smaller. March was the most difficult month of the year. The food barrels were almost empty. The animals that gave milk were themselves starving. People were ill from lack of fruits and vegetables. Finding the strength to plant the spring crops was almost impossible. Still, come April, folks all across the land would somehow muster the energy to begin the cycle of planting once again. The surest sign that spring had come was the sight of the colonists bent over, making thousands of small hills, poking a hole in the top of each one, and dropping life-giving corn seeds inside.

SURPRISING HISTORY

Moon-gardening? Many colonists believed the moon was the key to a successful harvest and a well-fed winter. People looked to the moon for the best time to slaughter their animals and plant their crops, split their logs and pick their fruit. For example, it was thought best to kill a cow under a full moon, since the "meat would be sweeter."

Fireplaces were used every day, all year round. In time, sooty deposits in the chimneys could cause fires. In some towns, settlers would sometimes drop a chicken down their chimneys. Its frantic wing-beating would clean up some of the soot!

Let's say you don't want to clean your room or do your homework. Wouldn't it be great to get someone else to do those hard jobs for you? Maybe you've even threatened your sister or brother and gotten him or her to do your chores. If you have, you have had an experience with servitude.

THE LAND OF THE FREE?

That's what we call America. But the truth is, this country was built on the sweat and hard work of people who were forced to do jobs they did not want to be doing.

Slavery wasn't invented in America. Slavery has been around for almost as long as people. But how could it have existed in a country whose motto would one day be "all men are created equal"?

How did slavery get its start? When wars were fought and people captured, they had to be fed and clothed. It seemed only fair that they should do some work in return. This was the way things had been for thousands of years all over the world. America was no different. When the Spanish explorers started to criss-cross the continent, some Native Americans found themselves chained at the neck, hauling the Spaniards' things. They became the first slaves in the New World. But they were soon joined by a boatload of Africans who arrived in Jamestown in 1619.

FROM SERVANTS TO SLAVES

Some people spent their whole lives as slaves. But in the early days of the colonies, many people agreed to become a "slave" for a period of several years in exchange for land. Those people were called indentured servants (those first Jamestown Africans were indentured laborers). They worked without pay for four to seven years in exchange for food and shelter. In the end, they were supposed to receive land, a bushel of corn, some tools, and a new suit of clothes. There was only one problem: Most never lived long enough to claim their prize.

Even though so many were dying, the landowners found themselves giving away an awful lot of land to those who somehow survived their period of indenture. They realized that they needed more people to work on their rapidly growing farms and, especially, on their tobacco plantations. They needed people they would owe nothing to, *ever.*

No matter how hard life was, mothers still found time to hug and cuddle with their children. Sadly, though, families were often split apart and sent to work in different places.

TAKEN FROM AFRICA
★

Picture this: You have gone for a walk in the woods. Suddenly, a huge net is dropped down on you from a tree. Strangers come and tie you up before you can escape. Within weeks, you will find yourself on a ship, pitching and rolling across a vast ocean…taken from your family…alone and frightened. Can you imagine how scary that must have been? Can you imagine how *you* would feel?

For hundreds of years, that was the fate of many an African. Today, it horrifies us to even think about it. But in times past, the buying and selling of people—slavery—was considered perfectly okay. The Portuguese were among the first to start kidnapping Africans with the help of other Africans. Wars were raging between rival tribes and some leaders figured that this was an easy way to get rid of their strongest enemies. The Portuguese built a huge fort, called "the Mine," on Africa's Gold Coast and packed it with thousands of young people, all between the ages of fifteen and twenty-five. Bound by chains, guns pointed at their heads, escape was impossible.

Greedy plantation owners decided to take a new approach. While indentured servants had to be given land at the end of their time of indenture, slaves did not. A slave's children and grandchildren, and all future generations, would forever belong to the plantation owners. Slaves provided an instant workforce for the spreading plantations. And slavery meant the plantation owners could keep all of their profits. To a plantation owner, the decision was simple. Slavery was now here to stay.

Still, some of the first Africans in the colonies earned their freedom. Some became sailors. Some even became plantation owners themselves!

A SAD DEVELOPMENT
★

We did not invent slavery here in America. What we *did* invent was the idea that one group of people should become property based on the color of their skin. America was entering into a terrible time…a time when all men were *not* created equal according to our laws. In the years to come, that was to be the way things were in a land where freedom was *supposed* to be a way of life.

BROUGHT TO AMERICA
★

Those slave traders would soon have many buyers for their captives. Ten years after the founding of Jamestown, plantation owners were discovering that growing tobacco was hard, dirty work—but work that was making them a ton of money. Word about how difficult life was on the plantations had spread back to England. It was brutally hot, there were bugs everywhere, and it was impossible to *not* get sick. Fewer and fewer indentured servants signed on.

One nation under God? Not in the early days of our country. It seemed that everybody had a different idea of how to worship. That would have been okay if people hadn't tried to force their opinions on everybody else. If you have ever wondered what the difference is between a Puritan and a Pilgrim, a Quaker and a Baptist—read on.

DEAR GOD!

Amazing! That's the only way to describe the impact religion had in shaping America into the land it is today. Nowadays, religion and government are two separate things. But four hundred years ago, religion *was* the government!

From the moment the first Spanish *conquistadores* arrived, they tried to convince the Native Americans that the Spanish way was the best way of praying. They built churches, called missions, all across the Americas and began spreading their message: The Roman Catholic Church was the one and only church. Millions of Native Americans were forced to give up their beliefs.

The Spanish built fancy churches all across their territories. These were built to impress the Native Americans—to make them think that the Christian God was more powerful than their spirits. This church, built in the late 1600s in Arizona, is called St. Xavier del Bac.

FIGHTING ABOUT FAITH
★

The settlers of Jamestown belonged to the Church of England. The Pilgrims, who were Separatists, hated the Church of England. Maryland was settled by English Catholics. The Church of England had broken away from the Catholic Church. The Massachusetts Bay Colony was led by Congregational Puritans who thought the Separatists had it all wrong. The new colonies were getting off to a rocky start—all because of religion.

Other new arrivals were bringing different ways of worshipping with them, such as the Dutch Reformed Church that grew in New York. Suddenly, there were lots of new ways to pray.

GO TO CHURCH ...OR ELSE!

★

In many of the early settlements, church attendance was a must. In Jamestown, not only did you have to go on Sunday, you had to go every day, twice a day. Sunday was a day when you stayed in church almost *all* day. If you missed services, you could be fined. In some places, if you missed church more than three times, you could be whipped! People did not miss church in the 1600s…EVER.

PURE PURITANS

★

Ten years after the Pilgrims, who were Puritans, arrived at Plymouth, the Massachusetts Bay Colony was born. Another boatload of Puritans had come to America, but they saw things differently from the Separatist Pilgrims. The new arrivals were very strict and frowned on things that were fun…like dancing and partying. After all, that took time away from working and praying.

Some people thought that the church was making too many demands on them—demands that had less to do with loving God than keeping the church running. Back in England, George Fox started a group called the Society of Friends. But everyone soon called them Quakers, because they sometimes shook with the intensity of their praying. They hated the idea of violence. How could you hurt anyone simply because they didn't share your beliefs? They started the colony of Pennsylvania, a place where all religions were accepted.

Dunking stools were used to "soak" the truth out of suspected witches by the Puritans. Held underwater for long periods, many people drowned.

The Quakers weren't the only ones who thought that the Puritans had gotten religion "wrong." A Puritan minister named Roger Williams also left to start a new colony where people could worship freely. He called it Rhode Island and eventually he founded the Baptist Church. Others were drawn to his colony. The first Jewish synagogue in America was built there in 1658. Religion brought comfort to people struggling in strange new places. And slaves, who suffered so much, found hope in the Bible, along with the brief rest church gave from work.

THE PRICE OF NOT BELIEVING

★

For some, religion could be very painful. A common punishment was branding, and folks who dared to believe something different were liable to wear their beliefs on their hands. Some, like the Quakers, had the letter *H* (for heretic, a word that means nonbeliever) burned into their skin. Other crimes merited different letters. *B* meant you were a blasphemer—someone who didn't agree with what the church was saying. And hands weren't the only things branded. Cheeks were, too! "Do unto others…" seemed a forgotten lesson.

THE WITCHES OF SALEM

In the summer of 1692, in Massachusetts, a minister's sermons about the devil turned deadly. When a few teenaged girls went into "fits," the people of Salem became convinced that the devil and his helpers—witches—were responsible. Soon, cries of "WITCH" filled the air.

Eventually, more than 100 people were accused of devil worship. Fifty "confessed," twenty-nine were found guilty, and nineteen were hanged! Too late, the townspeople realized that they had made a dreadful mistake.

Some people from the 1600s have become legends. But what really happened when the Europeans first came to the New World?

Were these men and women really brave and valiant heroes? Are their stories...

TRUTH...OR LIE?

Could you do something if you knew it would make you unpopular? Could you forgive someone and help them, even if they did something to harm you? Meet some people who did all that and more!

THE AMAZING ADVENTURES OF JOHN SMITH

—★—

Wild and dangerous—that was John Smith's life. He left home at the age of sixteen to find his fortune. Instead, he found himself fighting a war. He was wounded in battle, captured, and sold as a slave, but he escaped and managed to return home.

After that adventure, coming to America seemed like tame stuff. Naturally, it wasn't. Soon after arriving, Smith and a group of men were captured by the Powhatans. His comrades were all killed, but the chief was impressed by Smith's bravery and spared him. Did Pocahontas, the chief's eleven-year-old daughter, save Smith's life? Probably not! Smith said nothing about it at the time, and only mentioned it many years later.

At any rate, Smith was released and allowed to return to Jamestown, where he found his fellow settlers at their wit's end. He told the lazy "gentlemen" that if they didn't start working, they wouldn't get anything to eat! Smith was bossy and loud, and when he talked—well, yelled—people listened!

A few months later, a gunpowder explosion left Smith seriously injured. He returned to England to recover, but in time he did come back to America. This time he headed north to Maine and Massachusetts!

The truth? He was an able leader of the Jamestown settlers and helped them get organized. The lie? His tale about being saved by Pocahontas was a *tall* tale, told to impress his friends.

POCAHONTAS— PRINCESS OF PEACE?

—★—

Just a few months before John Smith and his men arrived at Jamestown, a shaman—a wise man—warned the Powhatan chief that a nation would arise that would shatter his empire. The Powhatans went out and wiped out a nearby group of Chesapeakes, just to be on the safe side. But the real threat to their future was sailing across the Atlantic— the men and boys who were coming to build Jamestown. The link that bound the new colonists to the Powhatans would be the chief's daughter, Matoaka, a lively girl who had been nicknamed Pocahontas, which means "naughty child."

She did *not* throw herself between her father's club and John Smith's head. What *did* happen was that she was kidnapped by the colonists when she was about sixteen and held hostage to keep peace between the colonists and the Powhatans. John Rolfe, a settler whose wife and baby had died on the way over from England, took a liking to her. They were married and Matoaka changed her name to Rebecca, had a son named Thomas, and eventually went to England with Rolfe. The damp English weather did not agree with her. She died in London at the age of twenty-one.

The truth? Her friendliness with the Europeans ended up with them taking advantage of her. The lie? Pocahontas did not put her life on the line for John Smith. In fact, when she met up with him in London many years later, she called him a liar!

THE PILGRIMS AND THE ROCK

★

Visitors to Plymouth flock to see the rock where the Pilgrims supposedly set foot on American soil for the first time. It's not very big. Actually, it's a little disappointing. And the Pilgrims probably never set foot on it!

This is how the legend got its start: In 1741, a six-year-old boy named Ephraim Spooner happened to be on the beach at the same time as a ninety-five-year-old man named Thomas Faunce was being pushed in his wheelchair along the seashore. Spooner overheard the old man telling someone that he had been told by *his* father, who had heard it from a sailor, that the Pilgrims had made their first landing at Plymouth on a rock. The elderly Faunce raised a trembling hand, pointed at a big boulder on the beach, and said, "That rock!" The truth? Ships avoid rocks. They don't tie up alongside them. The whole legend is based on a child's memory of an old man's recollections.

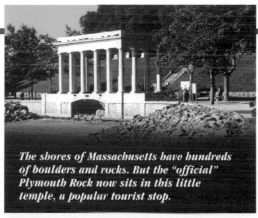

The shores of Massachusetts have hundreds of boulders and rocks. But the "official" Plymouth Rock now sits in this little temple, a popular tourist stop.

SQUANTO'S TALE

★

His real name was Tisquantum, but we know him as Squanto—a young man who was kidnapped by English explorers 15 years before the Pilgrims came to America. He was brought to England, like a captured zoo animal. But his tremendous dignity earned him the friendship of Sir Ferdinando Gorges—one of the heads of the Plymouth Company. Squanto found himself serving as a guide for seafarers mapping the New World.

In 1614, Squanto was recaptured by English traders and was about to be sold as a slave when he was rescued by a group of monks who wanted to convert the Native Americans to Christianity. He lived with them for four years, but he longed to return to his homeland.

And what did he find upon his return? His entire village abandoned—most of the group dead from the Europeans' dreaded diseases.

Brokenhearted, Squanto joined another Wamponoag group, headed by the great chief Massasoit. When a boatload of Europeans arrived and settled on the site of Squanto's old village, he was sent to spy on the newly arrived Pilgrims. Instead, Squanto befriended them. Without his help, they never would have survived. Squanto arranged a peace treaty between the newcomers and the Native Americans, and helped them learn to fish and farm. He died of a fever in his early twenties. The truth? Squanto became a very powerful person and sometimes took advantage of that power with both the Pilgrims and the Wamponoag to increase his own fortunes.

Did Squanto teach the Pilgrims to fertilize their corn with herrings? Some historians now say the English already knew how to do that.

Back and forth across the seas, the ships came and went,
bringing new people to America's shore and carrying the treasures of
the New World back to Europe.

GIVE AND TAKE

For many years, perhaps even before Columbus made his famous trip, fishermen had known about the fish-rich waters of the Atlantic. They kept it a secret because they didn't want anyone else to know about their special fishing spots. One sailor said that the fish practically jumped onto the boats! The fishermen knew what the new settlers soon found out. America was chock-full of all sorts of wonderful natural resources.

SMOKE SIGNALS
★

Today, we know that smoking can kill you. But in the 1600s, people actually believed that tobacco was good for their health. Doctors prescribed it when folks got sick. That belief would save the colony of Jamestown.

Tobacco was Virginia's first cash crop. Almost every Native American group smoked pipes as part of their religion. In fact, Columbus's ships were met by Arawak Indians smoking long pipes they called *tobagos*. That's how those brown crumbled leaves got their name. Spanish and French explorers brought tobacco to Europe in the mid 1500s, and in 1585 Sir Walter Raleigh brought pipe smoking to the court of the Queen. Smoking became "cool." Everyone did it.

The climate in America's South was perfect for growing tobacco. John Rolfe (who eventually married Pocahontas) managed to "borrow" some tobacco seeds from a Spanish gentleman and in 1615, the Jamestown settlers sent their first barrels of tobacco to Europe. Their crops were a huge success. In fact, for a long time, tobacco was used as money!

FISH TALES
★

There were more riches just waiting to be reeled in. The waters of the Atlantic were teeming with fish, and by 1665 there were three hundred huge boats and over 1,300 smaller ones trawling for fish. The best fish—cod and mackerel—got dried and salted and sent to Spain and Portugal. The worst got sent to the Caribbean to feed slaves. Fishing was so important that if you were a fisherman you didn't have to serve in the militia during fishing season.

HOW MUCH WOOD COULD A WOODCHUCK CHUCK?

★

America was covered by huge forests. To the new settlers from England—a land with almost no forests—all that wood meant salvation. They had something the Europeans needed. Trees!

It took great quantities of wood to build a ship and ships were the key to controlling the world. The mightier a country's navy, the more powerful it was. In the northernmost parts of New England, trees that soared as high as ten-story buildings were perfect for ships' masts and the first crop sent from Plymouth was a boatload of wood!

Back then, people also used wood to heat their homes. It took 140 bushel baskets of coal—coal made from burning a huge pile of wood—to make a ton of iron. Barrel-makers needed wood for their casks. Leather-makers peeled bark off chestnuts or willows to get tannin to soften their hides. *Everyone* needed wood, and lots of it. By the end of the 1600s, every town in New England had a sawmill to cut trees into planks and boards to be shipped back to Europe.

Animal skins were another great American resource. The French and the Dutch were especially eager to trade in fur pelts, and many a hardy fur trader left the relative safety of towns and settlements to venture deeper into America's heartland. They traded bear and fox, wolf and racoon—even skunk. If it was a decent-sized animal and it had fur, the Europeans wanted it!

IN GOOD COMPANY

Parts of America were settled by big businesses. They hoped for huge profits, but in the end they were all disappointed.

THE DUTCH WEST INDIES COMPANY explored and settled much of what is now New York.

THE PLYMOUTH COMPANY put up the money for the Pilgrims' journey.

THE VIRGINIA COMPANY financed Jamestown and several other Virginia settlements.

Do you remember the rhyme about the butcher, the baker, and the candlestick-maker? Well, there were plenty of jobs to be done in the early settlements. Big jobs. Hard jobs. Important jobs. And some very odd jobs, too.

RICH MAN, POOR MAN

Work. Work. Work. Every day was filled with it. Some folks had skills they brought with them from Europe. Others had to learn how to do things they had never done before.

This cooper, or barrel-maker, is working at a "shaving horse." A foot pedal operates a clamp that holds the wood tightly while a sharp knife cuts or shapes it.

FROM BLACKSMITHS TO BASKETWEAVERS
★

SURPRISING HISTORY

Today when you need something, you might dash over to the mall. But for about 40 years there were no stores in America. The first shop opened up in Salem, Massachusetts, 30 years after the Pilgrims arrived. The owner sold everything from locks to knives to elegant silk fabrics. He even sold children's toys!

In Europe there were shops where you could buy things. But as new arrivals poured onto America's shores, they were sometimes surprised to find that if they wanted something, in most cases they had to make it themselves. Some people put their skills to use right away.

Blacksmiths were one of the most needed craftspeople. They made nails for building homes, hooks for hanging clothes, and hinges so doors could open and close. Horses needed horseshoes. Home builders needed axes. Blacksmiths made and repaired all these. Whitesmiths worked with finer metals, like pewter and silver.

Every home needed baskets, so basket makers wove willows and tall grasses into different weaves, perfect for gathering greens from the garden, or storing corn and grain. And one of the most important people, especially in the port towns of Boston, New York, and Charleston, was the cooper. It was his job to make the barrels that were used to send products back to Europe.

In the colonies' early days, these folks stayed busy as bees.

MONEY DOESN'T GROW ON TREES
★

In America's early days money grew in the ground and could be found lying around on the beach. Early settlers often paid with "stuff"—things like vegetables, tobacco, and cows. And everybody used the Native Americans' money—wampum— which was most often a circle-shaped bead made from either the shell of a periwinkle or a black clam called a quahog. Six periwinkles equaled an English penny. You could even pay for a college education with it. Harvard took it for tuition money!

Spanish pieces of eight were another type of money that was welcomed everywhere. They were called that because each coin was worth eight reals—another type of Spanish currency. (Confused? It's very much like our quarters, four equal a dollar.) The neatest thing about these coins was that a "piece" of a piece of eight was worth whatever fraction of the coin had been broken off. The littlest bits were called, not surprisingly, bits. Two bits equaled a quarter. To this day some people refer to our quarters as two bits.

During the second half of the 1600s, different colonies tried minting their own money, but none of the colonies really trusted each other. Coins were easy to duplicate. And although money didn't grow on trees, it was too easy to make a fake.

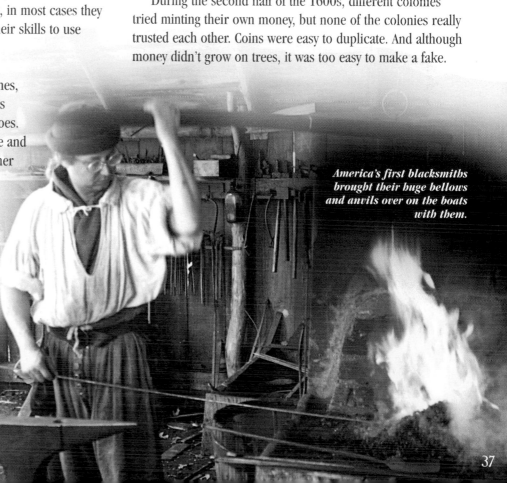

America's first blacksmiths brought their huge bellows and anvils over on the boats with them.

Take a bit of France and add a big chunk of Spain. Stir in hearty helpings of Sweden and Germany with a hunk of Holland, too. Add England and Scotland and Africa to the mix. Don't forget the Native Americans, who were here before everyone else. Now you've got the recipe for…

AMERICAN PIE

America brought many different worlds together. Windmills that would have been at home in Holland dotted the landscapes of Massachusetts and New York.

America drew people from all over the continent of Europe. Russians came along with the Dutch to New Amsterdam. People from Poland arrived on the same ship as Englishmen bound for Virginia. Frenchmen fell in love with Native American women and joined their groups. Africans came, sometimes as slaves, sometimes as free people. Each learned from the other, blotting up bits of culture like a paper towel mops up a spill.

WHAT'S NEW?

There were lots of "new" things in the New World. There was New France. New Netherland. New Scotland. New Spain. New Sweden. New England. But even though people called this the New World, they found that their old ways still had considerable value, and they were happy to share their customs with their new neighbors.

In Europe, travel between countries was rare. The English hadn't a clue as to how the Germans or the French or the Spanish lived. But in America, there might be a community of people from Finland just a few miles away from a town settled by the Dutch. In the port cities, as ships from a dozen different countries filled the harbors, a swirl of foreign languages filled the air— African slaves who spoke with Dutch accents…Germans with an Irish lilt to their speech.

Always learning. Always watching. Willing to try new things. Adapting old ways to new places. That became the American way.

SURPRISING HISTORY

Potatoes were native to the Americas. But the colonists hated them when they first arrived. They did send some potato plants to Europe, however, and the Scots and Irish took a quick liking to them. When those two groups came to America later on, they brought their "Irish" potatoes with them. And those soon became an all-American favorite.

AS AMERICAN AS...

★

Life was so hard in America, folks adopted whatever made life easier. The Swedish settlers brought small axes with them and amazed the English colonists by being able to take down a big tree in half the time two Englishmen with a saw needed to do the same thing. The Swedes' and Finns' log cabins

were warmer and sturdier than the English wattle and daub cabins. In time, log cabins became the house of choice for many a pioneer family.

In England, where there were few wild animals, fences weren't really necessary. But in America, where hungry wolves and coyotes were just waiting for a chance to snack on the nearest sheep or cow, you had to have a fence if you wanted to eat. The Germans quickly adapted the Native Americans' fences and improved on them slightly.

DUNKING DOUGHNUTS

★

Foods from far-off lands now became American favorites. The Dutch brought us doughnuts, waffles, cole slaw and, best of all, cookies, named for the Dutch *koekje*! Germans gave us hamburgers, sausages, and sauerkraut. The French gave us hearty soups called chowders. And the Spanish brought us fiery spices and chilies along with a delicious delicacy—hot chocolate!

SPEAKING AMERICAN-ESE

★

Dozens of different languages got mixed together in the New World. Today, when you speak English, you probably don't even realize that you are speaking a mush of many different tongues. Do "spooks" scare you on Halloween? That's the Dutch word for "ghost." The Dutch gave us a slew of other words, too—such as "yacht" and "boss" and "dope." Our modern-day Santa Claus comes from the Dutch "Sinterklaas," although we did fatten him up a bit in America!

DOLLARS AND SENSE

Nowadays we use the American dollar to buy things. But you'll be surprised to hear that our dollar was born in Germany. It got its name from a coin called a thaler. The actual name is *Joachimsthaler*, but as you can imagine, no one ever called it that!

Oddly, it was the Spanish who first brought these coins to America. From about 1690 on, the thaler and the Spanish piece of eight became one and the same. When America started minting its own money, the name stuck.

FROM AFRICA'S COASTS

★

Many Africans were fine fishermen and seafarers. They contributed heavily to the fishing industries in North and South Carolina—sharing boat-building and net-making skills with the English settlers. They also taught the colonists how to kill the crocodiles that were tormenting them.

HOME ON THE RANGE

★

The Spanish presence is felt most strongly in America's Southwest. New Mexico saw the first permanent Spanish settlement in North America, started in 1610. The Spaniards used the vast lands for raising cattle and sheep to sell in the bigger Spanish towns in Mexico. And there, in America's West, the first cowboys rode the ranges. Their lifestyle inspired those hard-riding, steer-roping, ranch-owning cowpokes who became an American legend.

Hot stuff! When the Spaniards settled in the Southwest, they quickly took to the Native Americans' red-hot cooking and soon put their own unique spin on it.

Imagine a leaking roof—just an occasional drip falls every once in a while in the beginning. But soon it starts dripping more and more. Water starts pouring in too fast, filling the buckets placed underneath, finally overflowing onto the floor—a big, messy flood. That's what happened when the Europeans first came to America. A trickle of people became a flood that threatened to wash away the people who were already here. The only way to stop that flood was…

A FIGHT TO THE DEATH

What were the Native Americans to do? The Europeans had changed everything. Their diseases had killed off three-quarters of the Native Americans. The new colonies were growing bigger and bigger as more and more people sailed over from Europe, pushing into the Native Americans' territories. There were bad feelings between the two groups. There was only one possible way for this story to end. *War!*

Now, some Europeans had been fair in their dealings with the Native Americans. Some had treated them with respect and dignity. But others had taken advantage of the Native Americans and then turned on them. That betrayal led to bloodshed.

And that wasn't the only fighting going on. The French and English, at war in Europe, carried their hatred across the ocean to America's shores, involving the Native Americans in their endless battles with one another.

Burning villages. Bloody deaths. Orphaned babies crying in the dark. Weeping wives burying their dead husbands. Too often, that was what America looked like.

There was great cruelty on both sides. The Native Americans scalped their victims. The Europeans chopped off the heads of their enemies and carried them around on sticks. The saddest part was that most of the fighting could have been avoided. Much of it was started by misunderstandings.

I WANT YOUR LAND!

★

In 1637, a Puritan army from the Massachusetts Bay Colony marched along the Mystic River in Connecticut, into the main village of the Pequot nation, and burned the homes of hundreds of men, women, and children. They were helped by a rival group—the Narragansett—longtime enemies of the Pequot, after the Puritans promised they wouldn't harm the women and children. But that proved to be a lie. More than six hundred Pequots died that day. Most were mothers and small children. And soon, scenes like this were repeated over and over again. America was heading into a century of war—too many wars where too many died.

Along the lower Hudson River, more than a thousand Native Americans and hundreds of Dutch colonists died during Governor Kieft's War, which began after the Dutch governor of New Netherland decided to tax the Native Americans. But the bloodiest fighting took place when a Wampanoag leader named Metacom, whom the English for some reason had named King Philip, decided he had had enough of the colonists' slow, steady stealing of his lands.

John Underhill lead the Puritans in the deadly battle with the Pequots. When it was over, the few Pequots who survived were enslaved and forbidden to ever mention their tribe's name again.

How terrifying it must have been for all those who managed to survive the fighting. Mothers and fathers dead…no place to lay your head at night…all alone and so very sad.

KING PHILIP'S WAR

★

Fifty years after the Pilgrims landed in Plymouth, there were more than 40,000 colonists in New England alone. Metacom (King Philip) knew he had to do something to stop the Europeans or his nation would be lost. He got several other groups to join his cause and together they attacked more than 50 English settlements, completely destroying a dozen, and scaring the daylights out of the colonists. For a year, they waged a war of terror and swift attack, but their numbers were too small and the colonists' guns too strong. Metacom was finally captured and killed, his head chopped off and stuck on a pole in the center of Plymouth—a tragic end for a brave leader.

WAR HEADS

★

Throughout the 1600s, the French, the English, and the Spanish acted like spoiled, stubborn preschoolers fighting over a toy they all wanted. The French had managed to develop some trust with the Native Americans, and convinced many groups to join their side. In the years to come, battles would erupt in almost every colony in America. King William's War lasted for eight long years and saw French-led Native American attacks throughout New England and New York. A truce lasted for five years before it all blew up again in Queen Anne's War. All that ever really changed were the names of the kings and queens. The end result was always the same—death and despair.

SURPRISING HISTORY

War paint was an important part of the Native American's fighting style. The reason they were called "red men" by the Europeans was because they used to cover themselves with bear fat that had red coloring mixed in with it. Stripes and dots of black made them look extra fierce.

Almost four hundred years later, their words reach out to us, across the centuries. These are the actual thoughts and feelings of people just like you, people who dreamed big dreams and longed for happiness and good fortune.

IN THEIR OWN WORDS

"THE LAST THING IN THEIR MINDS WAS TO HARM US"

★

Jaques Lemoyne de Morgues was a French colonist who tried to start a settlement in Florida in 1565. It did not last. Spanish soldiers marched in and killed almost everyone. He was one of the few survivors. This is part of his memory of the colonists' first meeting with the Native Americans.

"We found the seashore crowded with native men and women who kept up very large fires. At first we thought it necessary to be on guard against them, but very soon we realized that the last thing in their minds was to harm us…they gave numerous proofs of their friendly intentions. They brought us grains of roasted maize, ground into flour, or whole ears of it, smoked lizards or other wild animals which they considered great delicacies, and various kinds of roots, some for food, others for medicine."

"WE SHALL ALL BE DESTROYED"

★

Miantonomi was a member of the Narragansett nation that was located in what is now Connecticut and Rhode Island.

"Brothers, we must be one as the English are, or we shall all be destroyed. You know our fathers had plenty of deer and skins and our plains were full of game and turkeys, and our coves and rivers were full of fish. But brothers, since these Englishmen have seized our country, they have cut down the grass with scythes and the trees with axes. Their cows and horses eat up the grass, and the hogs spoil our beds of clams…and finally we shall starve to death. Therefore, I ask you, resolve to act like men."

"I ASKED THEM IF WE WERE NOT TO BE EATEN BY THOSE WHITE MEN"

★

Olaudah Equiano was eleven years old when he was kidnapped from his home in Nigeria and brought to the New World as a slave. Here is what he wrote about his first sight of the ship that would take him away from his home.

"When I looked around the ship and saw a large furnace of copper boiling, and a multitude of black people of every description chained together, every one of their countenances expressing dejection and sorrow, I no longer doubted my fate. Quite overpowered with horror and anguish, I fell motionless on the deck and fainted. When I recovered a little, I found some black people about me, and I believe some were those who had brought me on board and had been receiving their pay. They talked to me in order to cheer me up, but all in vain. I asked them if we were not to be eaten by those white men with horrible looks, red faces, and long hair. They told me I was not."

"BY THE GOODNESS OF GOD, WE ARE SO FAR FROM WANT"

★

Edward Winslow came to America aboard the Mayflower *when he was twenty-five years old. He helped found the Plymouth Colony and served as its governor three different times. This is his account of the first Thanksgiving feast—one of only two written descriptions that survive.*

"Our harvest being gotten in, our governor sent four men on fowling, that we so might after a special manner rejoice together after we had gathered the fruits of our labors. They four in one day killed as much fowl as, with a little help beside, served the company almost a week. At which time, amongst other recreations…many of the Indians coming amongst us, and among the rest, their greatest king Massasoit, with some ninety men whom for three days we entertained and feasted, and they went out and killed five deer, which they brought to the plantation and bestowed on our governor, and upon the captain and others. And although it be not always so plentiful as it was at this time with us, yet by the goodness of God, we are so far from want we often wish you partakers in our plenty."

SURPRISING HISTORY

How amazing is it that any writings survived for four hundred years? Very! Especially when you realize that only about 65 percent of the colonists could read and very few of them could write. John Winthrop, a governor of the Massachusetts Bay Colony, even noted in his journal that reading and writing too much had driven one woman insane. Learning to read so you could study the Bible was fine. Writing more than an occasional note was considered a waste of time.

Who says you can't travel through time? Well…you may not be able to zap yourself into the future, but you can zip back a few hundred years to chat with the Pilgrims and chase after their chickens. You can see pirates with swords swinging, racing through the streets of St. Augustine, and try your hand at ninepin on Jamestown's packed-earth streets. Cover your ears when the mighty cannons roar. You're about to take…

A STEP BACK IN TIME

Even though almost four hundred years have passed since the first colonists made the long sea journey to America, you can still see the world as it was way back then. All across America, living history museums have re-created the world of our ancestors.

JAMESTOWN, VIRGINIA
★

Most of the original site of the first permanent English settlement has been washed away by the James River, but close by, a replica of that first village will whisk you back to 1612. You can board re-creations of the ships that brought the settlers here and tie some knots with the sailors. Inside the fort, "colonists" in the dress of the time will answer all your questions. Try playing some games, drawing water from the well, and learning how to shoot a matchlock musket! A great museum with a kids' discovery room rounds out the fun.

ST. AUGUSTINE, FLORIDA
★

America's first permanent European settlement took root here 45 years before the English arrived. The Spanish settlers left a big mark! There's a huge stone fort where soldiers fire cannons and a charming Spanish Quarter where *señoritas* and *señors*, dressed in the style of the time, share how life was lived back then. Special programs throughout the year reenact several thrilling events.

CARTER'S GROVE, VIRGINIA
★

Once home to over a thousand Africans, this living history site will bring you face to face with all the hardship—and occasional happiness—in a slave's life. Special events like weddings (do you know what "jumping the broom" means?) capture some of the happier moments as you see how the slaves lived, and how they triumphed over their harsh lives. Carter's Grove is near Williamsburg, Virginia.

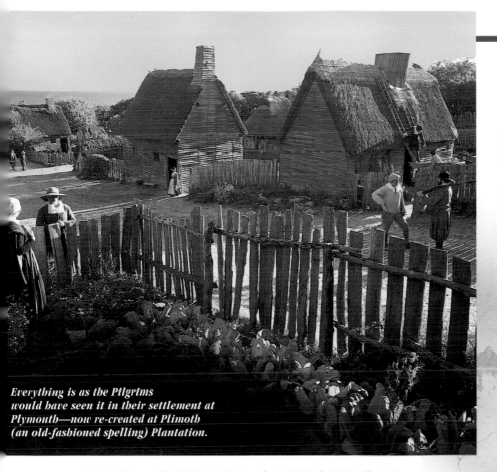

Everything is as the Pilgrims would have seen it in their settlement at Plymouth—now re-created at Plimoth (an old-fashioned spelling) Plantation.

ST. MARY'S CITY, MARYLAND
★

Set your watch back a few centuries as costumed interpreters bring you back to the 1640s. Help salt a ham on the foredeck of the sailing ship the *Dove*, and chat with the "captain." Then walk over to an early tobacco plantation and help "Mistress Godiah Spray" churn some butter and feed the biggest hogs you've ever seen!

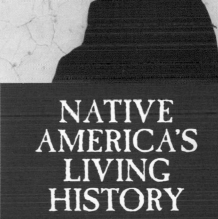

PLIMOTH PLANTATION, MASSACHUSETTS
★

As you pass through the fort gates and amble down over the rough path that leads to the sea, you'll be greeted by the men and women who came over on the *Mayflower* (actually, very talented actors and actresses who play their parts). They dress and speak in the style of the 1600s, so much in character that if you ask them a question about the present, they will stare at you blankly and say they don't understand. You can visit their houses and hear their stories. And you, too, can become an actor in this wonderful "play." Special Thanksgiving events let you celebrate 1600s-style! There's also a fine museum as well as a re-created Native American homestead (see box at right).

NATIVE AMERICA'S LIVING HISTORY

Glimpses of Native American life can still be seen. HABBOMOCK'S HOMESITE in Plimoth Plantation and the POWHATAN VILLAGE at Jamestown offer costumed interpreters just waiting to answer your questions. They go about their tasks as the Native Americans would have, making canoes, tanning hides, weaving baskets, and cooking. Another fascinating spot is the MASHANTUCKET PEQUOT MUSEUM AND RESEARCH CENTER in Mystic, Connecticut, which has a huge walk-through re-creation of a 1600s Pequot village.

45

As the sun set on the very last day of the very last year of the 1600s, nobody in America could guess what the new century would bring. People did not know that their quiet villages and sleepy towns would soon be changed forever. There would be fighting. There would be sacrifice. And there would be the proud birth of a new nation, as Americans went...

LOOKING FOR LIBERTY

So much had changed since the Europeans had come to the New World and all in such a short time. There were towns growing into cities and farms growing into plantations. Every day more and more people were crossing the Atlantic, heading westward to a land of plenty. But not everyone was prospering. The Native Americans were struggling to protect their territories— and their way of life. Thousands of Africans had been torn from their homelands and chained to a life of hurt and hate.

The story of this new America was only beginning. And as much as had changed in the first hundred years, the century to come would change things even more—changes that would alter the course of history!

WITH GRATEFUL THANKS

This book would not have been possible without the help and cooperation of many wonderful people and organizations. They are:

Carol City at Plimoth Plantation

Debby Padgett at the Jamestown-Yorktown Foundation

Cathy Grosfils at The Colonial Williamsburg Foundation

David Holahan at the Mashantucket Pequot Museum and Research Center

Very special thanks to my ever-patient children, Alex and Tish Scolnik, and my husband, Lou, who traveled with me to a fascinating place called America's past. Thanks also to Ms. Elizabeth Yohan's 5th grade history classes at the Increase Miller School.

READ MORE ABOUT IT

★

It is impossible to fit one hundred years into the pages of one book. Here are some titles that offer other glimpses of this fascinating century:

Dear America: A Journey to the New World:
The Diary of Remember Patience Whipple, *Mayflower*, 1620
by Kathryn Lasky; Scholastic, 1997

Brown Paper School USKids History:
Book of the American Colonies
by Howard Egger-Bovet and Marlene Smith Baranzini;
Little, Brown and Company, 1996

The New England Indians
by C. Keith Wilbur; The Globe Pequot Press, 1993

A History of US: The First Americans
A History of US: Making Thirteen Colonies
by Joy Hakim; Oxford University Press, 1993

GO ONLINE TO THE PAST

★

There are dozens of wonderful Web sites that focus on American history. These are but a few:

This site will take you to Web locations which feature a walking tour of Plimouth Plantation. It will also whisk you to Jamestown, the early Spanish Missions, and many other fascinating sites:
http://www.jacksonesd.k12.or.us/k12projects/jimperry/colony.html

This link provides an excellent timeline of the major events of the 1600s and includes early voyages by European explorers:
http://www.historyplace.com/unitedstates/revolution/early.html

African-American history is at your fingertips. This site will take you to several different Web locations that focus on slavery and on the experiences of free Blacks in colonial times:
http://www.seacoastnh.com/blackhistory/hotlinks.html

Native American history can be found at many locations on the Web. This will lead you to some of the best sites:
http://www.ilt.columbia.edu/k12/naha/nanav.html

PHOTO CREDITS

★

INDEX